First published in Great Britain in 1996 by
BROCKHAMPTON PRESS,
20 Bloomsbury Street,
London WC1B 3QA.
A member of the Hodder Headline Group

This series of little gift books was made by Frances Banfield, Andrea P. A.
Belloli, Polly Boyd, Kate Brown, Stefano Carantini, Laurel Clark, Penny Clarke,
Clive Collins, Jack Cooper, Melanie Cumming, Nick Diggory, John Dunne,
Deborah Gill, David Goodman, Paul Gregory, Douglas Hall, Lucinda Hawksley,
Maureen Hill, Dennis Hovell, Dicky Howett, Nick Hutchison, Douglas Ingram,
Helen Johnson, C.M. Lee, Simon London, Irene Lyford, John Maxwell, Patrick
McCreeth, Morse Modaberi, Tara Neill, Sonya Newland, Anne Newman, Grant
Oliver, Ian Powling, Terry Price, Michelle Rogers, Mike Seabrook, Nigel Soper,
Karen Sullivan and Nick Wells.

ISBN 1 86019 4176

A copy of the CIP data is available from the British Library
upon request.

Produced for Brockhampton Press by Flame Tree Publishing, a part
of The Foundry Creative Media Company Limited, The Long House,
Antrobus Road, Chiswick W4 5HY.

Printed and bound in Italy by L.E.G.O. Spa.

Just For You

HAPPY
BIRTHDAY

Illustrated by

Douglas Hall

A.R.C.A.

Selected by Karen Sullivan

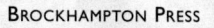

BROCKHAMPTON PRESS

My Birthday! 'How many years ago?
Twenty or thirty?' 'Don't ask me!'
'Forty or fifty?' 'How can I tell?
I do not remember my birth, you see!'
Julia Dorr, 'My Birthday'

❖

Time flies over us, but leaves its shadow behind.
Nathaniel Hawthorne

❖

With care, and skill, and cunning art,
She parried Time's malicious dart,
And kept the years at bay,
Till passion entered in her heart
And aged her in a day!
Ella Wheeler Wilcox

Our birthdays are feathers in the
broad wing of time.
Jean Paul Richter

Drink and dance and laugh and lie,
Love, the reeling midnight through,
For tomorrow we shall die!
(But, alas, we never do.)
Dorothy Parker

You have to count on living every single day in a
way you believe will make you feel good about
your life — so that if it were over tomorrow, you'd
be content with yourself.
Jane Seymour

A diplomat is a
man who always
remembers a
woman's birthday
but never remembers
her age.
Robert Frost

9

You know you're getting old when the candles cost more than the cake.
Bob Hope

A lady of a 'certain age', which means Certainly aged.
Lord Byron

When a man has a birthday, he may take a day off. When a woman has a birthday she may take as much as five years off.
E. C. McKenzie

Old age isn't so bad when you consider
the alternative.
Maurice Chevalier

Is it birthday weather for you, dear soul?
Is it fine your way,
With tall moon-daisies alight, and the mole
Busy, and elegant hares at play?
C. Day-Lewis, 'Birthday Poem for Thomas Hardy'

The thought of our past years in me doth breed
Perpetual benedictions.
William Wordsworth, Intimations of Immortality

He had hardly done so before the Professor was
back again, quite out of breath. 'Wishing you
many happy returns of the day, my dear child!' he
went on, addressing the smiling little girl, who
had run to meet him. 'Allow me to give you a
birthday-present. It's a second-hand pin-cushion,
my dear. And it only cost fourpence-halfpenny!'
'Thank you, it's *very* pretty!' And Sylvie
rewarded the old man with a hearty kiss.

'And the *pins* they gave me for nothing!' the
Professor added in high glee. 'Fifteen of 'em and
only one bent.'

Lewis Carroll, *Sylvie and Bruno*

. . Beyond the border and under
the lark full cloud
There could I marvel
My birthday
Away but the weather turned round.
Dylan Thomas, 'Poem in October.'

◈

To me, old age is always fifteen years older
than I am.
Bernard Baruch

I send thee pansies while the year is young,
Yellow as sunshine, purple as the night;
Flowers of remembrance, ever fondly sung
By all the chiefest of the sons of light;
And if in recollection lives regret
For wasted days, and dreams that were not true,
I tell thee that the pansy 'streaked with jet'
Is still the heart's-ease that the poets knew.
Take all the sweetness of a gift unsought,
And for the pansies send me back a thought.'
Sarah Doudney, 'Thoughts.'

The older you get the stronger
the wind gets — and it's always in your face.
Jack Nicklaus

The old believe everything; the middle-aged suspect everything; the young know everything.
Oscar Wilde

❖

These are the soul's changes. I don't believe in ageing. I believe in forever altering one's aspect to the sun. Hence my optimism.
Virginia Woolf

❖

You must not pity me because my sixtieth year finds me still astonished. To be astonished is one of the surest ways of not growing old too quickly.
Colette

One is rarely an impulsive innovator after the age of sixty, but one can still be a very fine orderly and inventive thinker. One rarely procreates children at that age, but one is all the more skilled at educating those who have already been procreated, and education is procreation of another kind.
G. C. Lichtenberg

A cheque or credit card, a Gucci bag strap, anything of value will do. Give as you live.
Jesse Jackson

What Youth deemed crystal, Age finds out was dew.
Robert Browning

Birthdays are nice,
so long as you don't have too many.
Anonymous

The return of my birthday, if I remember it, fills
me with thoughts which it seems to be the general
care of humanity to escape.

Samuel Johnson

Believing hear, what you deserve to hear;
Your birthday as my own to me is dear . . .
But yours gives most; for mine did only hand
Me to the world; yours gave to me a friend.

Martial, *Epigrams*

What's a man's age?
He must hurry more, that's all;
Cram in a day what his youth took a year to hold.

Robert Browning

I'm sorry you are wiser,
I'm sorry you are taller;
I liked you better
foolish,
And I liked you better
smaller.
Aline Murray Kilmer,
'For the Birthday of a
Middle-Aged Child'

21

I am for those who believe in loose delights,
I share the midnight orgies
of young men,
I dance with the dancers and
drink with the drinkers.
Walt Whitman

There are many paths to
the top of the mountain,
but the view is always
the same.
Chinese proverb

Giving presents is a talent; to know what a person wants, to know when and how to get it, to give it lovingly and well. Unless a character possesses this talent there is no moment more annihilating to ease than that in which a present is received and given.

Pamela Glenconner

Age is not important, unless you are a cheese.

Anonymous

Now may the warming love of friends
Surround you as you go
Down the path of light and laughter
Where the happy memories grow.

Helen Lowrie Marshall

Reading, solitude, idleness, a soft and sedentary life, intercourse with women and young people, these are perilous paths for a young man, and these lead him constantly into danger.

Jean-Jacques Rousseau

✦

A man's as old as he's feeling,
A woman as old as she looks.

Mortimer Collins

✦

To the oldest person I know.

Birthday card inscription

Here lies interred in the eternity of the past, from whence there is no resurrection for the days — whatever there may be for the dust — the thirty-third year of an ill-spent life, which, after a lingering disease of many months sank into a lethargy, and expired, January 22nd, 1821, A. D. leaving a successor inconsolable for the very loss which occasioned its existence.

Lord Byron, Journal entry on his birthday

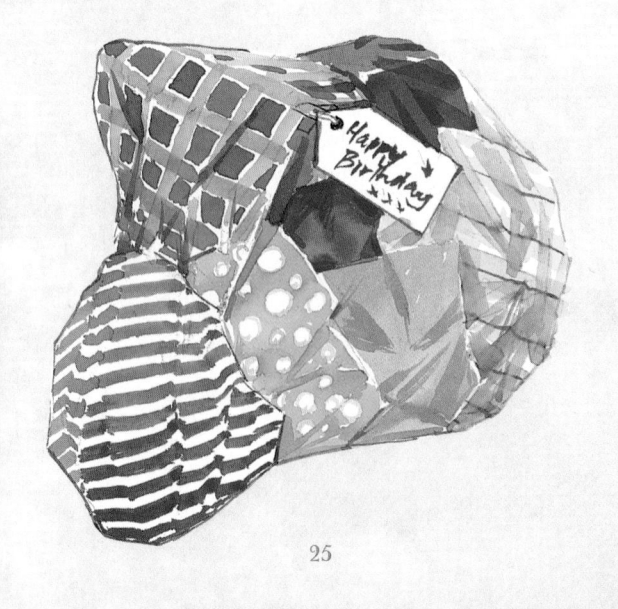

As life runs on, the road grows strange
With faces new, — and near the end
The milestones into headstones change,
'Neath every one a friend.
James Russell Lowell

May all the hairs on your head turn to
candles and light your way to heaven.
Irish birthday greeting

What should I say about life? That it's
long and abhors transparence.
Joseph Brodsky, on his fortieth birthday

To be seventy years young is sometimes far more cheerful and hopeful than to be forty years old.

Oliver Wendell Holmes Sr

Keep true the dreams of thy youth.

Friedrich von Schiller

Don't be sad
Don't be blue
I know someone
Older than you.

Birthday greeting

To divide one's life by years is of course to tumble into a trap set by our own arithmetic.

The calendar consents to carry on its dull wall-existence by the arbitrary timetables we have drawn up in consultation with those permanent commuters, Earth and Sun. But we, unlike trees, need grow no annual rings.

Clifton Fadiman, 'On Being Fifty'

One of the many things nobody ever tells you
about middle age is that it's such a nice change
from being young.

Dorothy Fisher

◈

Happy Birthday to you!
Violets are blue!
Roses are red!
Happy Birthday to you!

Traditional rhyme

◈

Age cannot wither her, nor custom stale
Her infinite variety.

William Shakespeare, *Antony and Cleopatra*

Thirty-five is a very attractive age.
London society is full of women of the highest
birth who have, of their own free choice, remained
thirty-five for years.
Oscar Wilde

All now was turned to jollity and game,
To luxury and riot, feast and dance.
John Milton, Paradise Lost'

Thirty — the promise of a decade of loneliness, a
thinning list of single men to know, a thinning
brief-case of enthusiasm, thinning hair.
F. Scott Fitzgerald, The Great Gatsby

How far that little candle throws his beams!

William Shakespeare, *The Merchant of Venice*

I can boast not wealth nor birth
Think you these alone have worth
Surely health, a heart that's true,
A hand that can protect you too,
Are gems, and these I proffer you.

Victorian birthday card inscription

Keeps dancing, music, and a feast,
To entertain a lovely guest.
John Fletcher, *The Faithful Shepherdess*

I dread no more the first white in my hair,
Or even age itself, the easy shoe,
The cane, the wrinkled hands, the special chair:
Time, doing this to me, may alter too
My sorrow, into something I can bear.
Edna St Vincent Millay, Sonnet

I am admonished in many ways that time is
pushing me inexorably along. I am approaching
the threshold of age; in 1977 I shall be 142.
This is no time to be flitting about the earth.
I must cease from the activities proper to youth
and begin to take on the dignities and gravities
and inertia proper to that season of honorable
senility which is on its way.
Mark Twain

Grow old along with me!
The best is yet to be,
The last of life, for which the first was made.
Robert Browning, 'Rabbi Ben Ezra'

Whatever poet, orator, or sage
May say of it, old age is still old age.
Henry Wadsworth Longfellow

There's a time when you have to explain to your
children why they're born and it's a marvellous
thing if you know the reason by then.
Hazel Scott

I am thirty-three — the age of the good Sans-culotte Jesus; an age fatal to revolutionists.

Camille Desmoulins

Since people are going
to be living longer and
getting older, they'll just
have to learn how to be
babies longer.
Andy Warhol

Ring a ring a roses,
A pocket full of posies,
Atishoo, atishoo,
We all fall down.

Fishes in the water,
Fishes in the sea,
We all jump up
With a one, two, three.
Traditional English nursery rhyme

Since it is the Other within us who is old, it is
natural that the revelation of our age should come
to us from outside — from others. We do not accept
it willingly.
Simone de Beauvoir

'Except ye become as little children', except you can wake on your fiftieth birthday with the same forward-looking excitement and interest in life that you enjoyed when you were five, 'ye cannot enter the kingdom of God'. One must not only die daily, but every day we must be born again.

Dorothy L. Sayers, 'Strong Meat'

One of the signs of passing youth is the birth of a sense of fellowship with other human beings as we take our place among them.

Virginia Woolf

Youth is not a question of years: one is young or old from birth.

Natalie Clifford Barney

The first thing which I can record concerning
myself is, that I was born . . . . These are
wonderful words. This life, to which neither time
nor eternity can bring diminution—this everlasting
living soul, began.
My mind loses itself
in these depths.
Margaret Oliphant

Oranges and lemons
Say the bells of St Clement's.
You owe me five farthings
Say the bells of St Martin's.
When will you pay me?
Say the bells of Old Bailey.
When I grow rich,
Say the bells of Shoreditch.
Pray when will that be
Say the bells of Stepney.
I do not know,
Says the great bell of Bow.
Here comes a candle to light you to bed.
Here comes a chopper to chop off your head.

Children's game

But it's hard to be hip over thirty
When everyone else is nineteen,
When the last dance we learned was the Lindy,
And the last we heard, girls who looked like
Barbra Streisand
Were trying to do something about it.
Judith Viorst

There is no cure for birth and death save to enjoy
the interval.
George Santayana

The value of old age depends upon the person who
reaches it. To some men of early performance it is
useless. To others, who are late to develop, it just
enables them to finish the job.
Thomas Hardy, Birthday Notes'

My time has been passed viciously and agreeably; at thirty-one so few years months days hours or minutes remain that 'Carpe Diem' is not enough. I have been obliged to crop even the seconds — for who can trust to tomorrow?
Lord Byron

Here we go round the mulberry bush,
the mulberry bush, the mulberry bush,
Here we go round the mulberry bush,
On a cold and frosty morning.
Children's game

Each day is a little life: every waking and rising a little birth, every fresh morning a little youth, every going to rest and sleep a little death.
Arthur Schopenhauer

I am six foot eleven.
My birthday covers
three days.
Darryl Dawkins

Enjoyed it! One more drink and I'd have been
under the host.
Dorothy Parker, when asked whether she enjoyed
a birthday party

Growing old is no gradual decline, but a series of tumbles, full of sorrow, from one ledge to another. Yet when we pick ourselves up we find no bones are broken; while not unpleasing is the new terrace which stretches out unexplored before us.
Logan Pearsall Smith

At age fifty, every man has the face he deserves.
George Orwell

One's prime is elusive. You little girls, when you grow up, must be on the alert to recognize your prime at whatever time of your life it may occur. You must then live it to the full.
Muriel Spark, *The Prime of Miss Jean Brodie*

It is not all bad, this getting old, ripening.
After the fruit has got its growth it should juice
up and mellow. God forbid I should live long
enough to ferment and rot and fall to the ground
in a squash.
Emily Carr

Look, I really don't want to wax philosophic, but
I will say that if you're alive, you got to flap your
arms and legs, you got to jump around a lot, you
got to make a lot of noise, because life is the very
opposition of death. And therefore, as I see it, if
you're quiet, you're not living. You've got to be
noisy, or at least your thoughts should be noisy
and colourful and lively.
Mel Brooks

The secret of staying young
is to live honestly,
eat slowly, and lie
about your age.
Lucille Ball

When you were born, you cried and the world
rejoiced. Live your life in such a manner that
when you die the world cries and you rejoice.
Indian Proverb

The closing years of life are like the end of
a masquerade party, when the masks are dropped.
Arthur Schopenhauer

The farmer's in his den,
The farmer's in his den,
Ee, ai, adio, the farmer's in his den.

The farmer wants a wife,
The farmer wants a wife,
Ee, ai, adio, the farmer wants a wife.
Children's game

Young men look forward
Old men look backward
The middle-aged look around.
English proverb

Somebody told me life is a waterwheel. It turns.
The trick is to hold your nose when you're under
it and not get dizzy when you're up.
James Baldwin, *Nobody Knows My Name*

I am not young
enough to know
everything.
Oscar Wilde

Middle age begins with the first mortgage and
ends when you drop dead.
Herb Caen

Life is a cup of
tea; the more
heartily we drink,
the sooner we reach
the dregs.

J. M. Barrie

There is not much comfort in life until one is old
enough to have the courage of his cussedness.

Don Herald

Lord Darlington: I wish I had known it was your birthday . . . I would have covered the whole street in front of your house with flowers for you. They are made for you.

Oscar Wilde, Lady Windermere's Fan

Man is like palm wine: when young sweet, but without strength; but in age, strong and harsh.

Congolese proverb

Age is opportunity no less,
Than youth itself, though in another dress,
And as the evening twilight fades away,
The sky is filled with stars, invisible by day . . .

Henry Wadsworth Longfellow

For every year of life we light
A candle on your cake,
To mark the simple sort of progress,
Anyone can make.

James Simmons, *In the Wilderness and Other Poems*

Growth is the only evidence of life.

Spanish proverb

53

After age seventy, it's patch, patch, patch.
Jimmy Stewart

Drink! Be merry!
Ring in the day
Happy Birthday to you!
Victorian song

A man who exposes himself when
he is intoxicated, has not the art
of getting drunk.
Samuel Johnson

There could I marvel my birthday.
Dylan Thomas, 'Deaths and Entrances'

Age is strictly a case of mind over matter. If you
don't mind, it doesn't matter.
Jack Benny

          ◈

As a white candle in a holy place
So is the beauty of an aged face.
Joseph Campbell, The Old Woman'

          ◈

This is my birthday,
this very day was Cassius born.
Shakespeare, *Julius Caesar*

          ◈

Because the birthday of my life
Is come, my love is come to me.
Christina Rossetti, 'A Birthday'

Our birth is but a sleep and a forgetting:
The Soul that rises with us, our life's Star,
Hath had somewhere its setting,
And cometh from afar.
William Wordsworth, 'Intimations of Immortality'

It was the afternoon of my eighty-first birthday,
and I was in bed with my catamite,
when Ali announced that the archbishop
had come to see me.
Anthony Burgess, *Earthly Powers*

You have honoured her fair birthday
with your virtues,
And as your due, you're hers.
William Shakespeare, *Two Noble Kinsmen*

At twenty the will rules,
At thirty the intellect,
At forty the judgement.
Baltasar Gracian proverb

Where my brother set
The laburnum on his birthday,
— The tree is living yet!
Thomas Hood, *I Remember*

❖

There could I marvel my birthday.
Dylan Thomas, *Deaths and Entrances*

❖

Only he that has travelled the road knows where
the holes are deep.
Chinese proverb

❖

Man, being reasonable, must get drunk;
The best of life is but intoxication.
Lord Byron

What a surprise!
I could just cry! . . .
'Happy Birthday, Lenny —
a Day Late' How cute!

Beth Henley, *Crimes of the Heart*

It was the Rainbow gave thee birth,
And left thee all her lovely hues.

W. H. Davies, *Farewell to Poesy*

It is my birthday.
I had thought t'have held it poor;
but since my Lord
Is Antony again, I will be Cleopatra.

Shakespeare, Antony and Cleopatra

❖

A man is as young as the woman he feels.

Groucho Marx

❖

On with the dance! let joy be unconfined;
No sleep till morn, when Youth and Pleasure meet
To chase the glowing hours with flying feet.

Lord Byron

❖

Acknowledgements:

The Publishers wish to thank everyone who gave permission to reproduce the quotes in this book. Every effort has been made to contact the copyright holders, but in the event that an oversight has occurred, the publishers would be delighted to rectify any omissions in future editions of this book. *Good News Study Bible,* published by Thomas Nelson, 1986, extracts reprinted with their kind permission; Dorothy Parker quotes from *The Best of Dorothy Parker,* first published by Methuen in 1952, reprinted by Gerald Duckworth & Co., © Dorothy Parker, 1956, 1957, 1958, 1959, renewed; Dylan Thomas, *Poem in October* published by J. M. Dent, reprinted courtesy of David Higham Associates; Simone de Beauvoir, reprinted courtesy of Weidenfeld and Nicholson and Andre Deutsch; D. H. Lawrence, from *The Complete Poems of D. H. Lawrence,* edited by Vivian de Sola Pinto and F. Warren Roberts, copyright © 1964, 1971 by Angelo Ravagli and C. M. Weekley, Executors of the Estate of Frieda Lawrence Ravagli. Used by permission of Laurence Pollinger Ltd and Viking Penguin, a division of Penguin Books USA Inc.; Virginia Woolf © The Estate of Virginia Woolf; Dorothy L. Sayers © the author's estate; Thomas Hardy reprinted courtesy of Penguin Books; J. M. Barrie, reprinted with the kind permission of Great Ormond Street Hospital; W. H. Davies, from *The Complete Poems of W. H. Davies,* published by Jonathan Cape, reprinted by kind permission of the Executors of the W. H. Davies Estate; C. Day Lewis, published by Jonathan Cape, reprinted by permission of A. D. Peters Ltd and The Executors of the Estate of C. Day Lewis; Muriel Spark was quoted in *The Penguin Dictionary of Modern Quotations,* by J. M. and M. J. Cohen.